Journey

Are you walking in your destiny???

By
Wanda Nance

Table of Contents

Introduction

Whether we are aware of it or not, our life is a journey. If we make the right journey with God we win here on earth, and our greatest reward is in heaven when we get to see Jesus face to face. Oh, what a day that will be!

"In My Father's house are many mansions," if it were not so, I would have told you I go to prepare a place for you. And if I go and prepare a place for you, I will come again and receive you to Myself; that where I am, there you may be also.
John 14:2-3

This book is going to take you through my journey in life and show you even in our worst times God is with us. It is never too late to get on the right path of life. You have not done anything too bad or been too good to be on God's journey for your life.
God gave us the Bible to be our guide through our journey of life. I love Abraham's journey. It wasn't easy from the very beginning. His name means Father of a

multitude and that was the promise God gave him also. The Lord told him to "Look now toward Heaven and count the stars if you are able to number them." God said, "So shall your descendants be." Abraham held on to that promise.

Abraham came from a heathen family and the first command God gave him was to move, to get out of his own country, from his family and from his father's house.

He should go to a land God will show him and God will bless him.

God didn't give him any details He just told him to go and Abraham obeyed the Lord. At this time he was around seventy-five years old. The age would have been enough to stop this generation. We would be too old and drawing a retirement check.

But as Abraham walked out his journey it took more faith at the end than it did when he first heard God. He also got wiser than he was at the beginning. When God promised him a son he hung on to that promise and told Sarah his wife. She in turn talked him into having a son with Hagar. That wasn't God's promise. Then he had to send Hagar and his son off because Sarah was jealous. How we try to figure out God's plans rather than wait on him to provide. When God speaks we think we need to make it happen. How crazy! God spoke the world into existence. But if it's not coming through let's help Him out. Or maybe that wasn't God after all. People, friends and family will start doubting you.   Not God of course but really was that God? When God said it was time to have a child with Sarah she was so old that she laughed about it.   She thought I'm too old now.

When God told Abraham to offer his son Isaac as a sacrifice, his only son of promise, he didn't tell anyone not Sarah not even Isaac. He just got up and obeyed. God wanted Abraham's heart, not Isaac's life. His obedience of faith earned him God's honor. Abraham was called friend of God.

Jesus said, "Ye are my friends if ye do whatsoever I command you."

Faith always has trials. The greater the faith the greater the trials. The greater the trial the greater the calling. So count it all joy!

Dedicated

I would like to dedicate this book to my two children. Amanda Shoemaker Martin, born 1981, and Joseph Austin Nance, born 1995, they have walked this journey of my life with me some things good and some not so well. Thanks, and I love you both more than words could ever tell.

A mother's love is the closest to unconditional love that we will ever know on this side of heaven.

<u>Acknowledgement</u>

I give Glory and Honor to Jesus Christ for all He has done for me and continues every day to love me. He is my best friend. He gives me this gift of writing and expressing how I feel. He has put people in my life and made me able to do what He has called me to do.

Special thanks to Mrs. Beverly Rhodes who has spent many hours proofreading my books. Without her my books are not possible.

I thank my children and grandchildren for always believing in me and for the sacrifice they have made for me to continue to write.

Special acknowledgement to Kathy Stephens, my friend and sister in Christ for the picture that she took of my granddaughter. It was used for the cover of this book.

Special thanks to each one of my brothers and sisters that share their testimony in hope that it will touch someone's life, Kenneth James, Stephanie Bell, Wendy Bailey, Lynda Atkins, and Genie Chadwick

My Child

Listening to the water run free,
Watching the sun glistering on the lake,
The wind blowing so hard against my
face,
The bright sun shining on me to keep
me warm,
God's glory surrounding me.
Sitting on a rock with broom straw   all
around me,
Recalling when I was a child wanting to
just
Run free!
In an open field filled with broom straw
and wild flowers.
Oh God, how you always restore our
soul,
If we will just sit in the quietness of
your beauty.
Be still, My Child, Be still!
And, wait upon me, I have your life
Planned out in the palm of my hand.
Be still and wait upon me!

My Journey
_1_

My journey of how the Lord had appointed me to be a minister and set the captives free so many years ago.

Thus saith God the Lord, he that created the heavens, and stretched them out; he that spread forth the earth, and that which cometh out of it; he that giveth breath unto the people upon it, and spirit to them that walk therein: I the Lord have called thee in righteousness, and will hold thine hand, and will keep thee, and give thee for a covenant of the people, for a light of the Gentiles; To open the blind eyes, to bring out the prisoners from the prison, and them that sit in darkness out of the prison house. I am the Lord: that is my name: and my glory will I not give to another, neither my praise to

graven images. Behold, the former things are
come to pass, and new things do I declare:
before they spring forth I tell you of them.
Isaiah 42:5-9

At the young age of twenty I thought I had it all together. But I was so far from the truth. I was a lost child of Gods. Who had my life planned out in the palm of His hand. He was starting my journey to become a minister some twenty-five years later.

Did He know all the wrong turns I was going to take? Yes, and He allowed me to take them. So from my life of mistakes, some wrong some right, I would be able to witness to so many different kinds of hurts that we go through in life. I look back and thank God for all I have been through, and it is evident that He was with me watching over me. He takes all our junk and makes a unique testimony for each one of us to go forth and be the minister He has called us to be.

At the age of twenty I started my journey. I moved from Mississippi to West Texas with Amanda, my three year old daughter. No job, just a hope with an ambition that I wanted to change my life, to better myself. I look back and think of the great faith I had. (My mom thought I was young and hard-headed)

I had driven in Jackson, Mississippi maybe a couple of time in my life. Before, I started on a journey of over eight hundred miles; I had no idea of direction, or how to read road signs. I went through Dallas/ Ft. Worth on I- 30 downtown on a Friday afternoon at five o'clock. (Scared to death). I had gripped the steering wheel, so tight I had fingernail marks in the palm of my hands. I got to my destiny around midnight. I was so tired, I was seeing things. I look back now and know it was part of my journey. That Monday morning I got a job at a bonding agency handling all municipal cases. They had court on the hour, and someone from the company had to be there. If your client didn't show up, you had seven days to get them in court or you pay the bond. That could run into a great liability really fast. The company was not even doing municipal bonds anymore until I started. I took the job and ran with it. I always like a challenge, and that was a great one. I was a little tom-boy from Mississippi with a great southern accent. I had never worn a dress but a few times, and that was to funerals. All the work I had ever done was in a sewing factory. I was a high school drop-out, and when my classmates graduated that bothered me, so I went and received my GED. This job was a great challenge for me and for the company. My employer had never had anyone to take this position. He offered it to me on a pay percentage fifty/fifty, which means I got half of the money that came in, but I also had to pay half if the client didn't show up. In that two years working for this company we lost very few bonds.

I remember going shopping that first weekend buying business clothes, high heels, dresses, and pantsuits. I loved it I was becoming someone with an identity. My boss would get tickled watching me. I had the drive in me. I would go to court, do the paper work, call the clients and even run down the clients that didn't show up for court. That's where the tom-boy part came in to work at my advantage. It didn't scare me, I liked it! I would run a client down in a heartbeat. I guess they thought a little women like me must have a mighty big gun or was just crazy. I remember one guy I   picked up with no problem. I brought him back to the office, and our bounty hunter was going to carry him across to the jail, and he ran on him. The boss and the guys in the office wouldn't let him live it down.

About six months after I had moved to Texas, I got married to Hampton. Everything was great we both made good money, and worked together. We even got married in the bonding company. I will never forget we had a shot gun wedding. The boss came in during the wedding with a shot gun to make sure I wanted this wedding. We finished working that day and flew out to San Antonio, Texas, for our honeymoon. It was all a great life style that I had never known. We ate at the tower in San Antonio, a restaurant that had a rotating floor four hundred and fifty feet in the air. We had life great at a very young age. Hampton and I did things that most people never get to do. We had four beautiful children together Jacqueline was six, Justin was four, Amanda was three, and Kristen was two. (talk about the Brady bunch). Shortly after we were married we started going to church. We enjoyed it. Life was good. I had never really gone to church that much when I was growing up, but I always felt judged because I came from a broken home. But this was different. Shortly after we had started going I gave my life to the Lord, but not really understanding I knew that I was different. I remember that day coming home from church lying on the couch feeling as if I could just float out the window. I always think back and know I was saved back then. We would go to church, Sunday school, Wednesday night service, give tithes, and we even went on a mission trip with the church to Mexico. We would pray over our meals and pray with the kids as we put them to bed.   But we never understood we were supposed to read the Bible and have a relationship with Jesus Christ. So of course Satan started moving in, and we were not prepared for his war. We would go to church and everything was great, and as soon as we left the fight was on. Satan was pushing our buttons, and we didn't know it! This went on for several years. We stayed in stagnate water, not growing in the Lord just in the church.

A little over a year working at this agency we were offered a company to buy. We were stepping out buying this company on a ninety day payoff of   Five thousand down which we borrowed from my mom. We were going to pay the other two payments of five thousand a month. We signed the papers for the company around nine that night, and by the next morning we paid her off. God is good! He was continuing blessing us. We worked around the clock, seven days a week. We would sleep at the office, and he would take two kids with him home, get dressed come back, and I would take the other two. We both were excited about our lives. We would all stay up at the office, and the kids would play and watch TV. Hampton was always videoing us. But when customers would come in the kids knew to go to the back room because it was work time.

One time we had customers up front and Jacqueline and Amanda were playing in the back room. When we heard this loud noise, we both went running to find Amanda lying on the floor with a file cabinet drawer on top of her head. I reached down and tossed it off her. (later I could not even move it).I grabbed her up with blood running down her head. It had cut her ear and her face had already turned black and blue. I rushed out the door to carry her to the hospital. Hampton had to stay until help got to the office. They took our information and told me to have a seat. In just a few minutes Hampton came in and demanded on somebody to help us. Then they called the police to make sure it wasn't child abuse. They had to put several stitches behind her ear. But she was okay, Praise God! The girls were playing house. They had pulled all sixteen cabinets out for them to crawl under and of course being top heavy they began to fall with Amanda under them. Praise God He was watching over my baby girl!
It's still amazing how we raised them in the office and worked around the clock. They knew when to be quiet and when to play. There was no outside playing because we were in downtown Odessa, Texas. And

Odessa was rated as one of the top ten crime cities in the United States. Business was good, but we also knew our kids weren't safe outside. One time Amanda and Jacqueline were playing at the back door in the snow, and one of our lawyer friends came up and told them to come inside. They wouldn't listen so he picked up a broom as if he was going to pop them with it. Amanda said, "I will tell my mommy, and she will fire you." She was around four at the time, and we had such a laugh over that.

Red, one of our employees, would buy all different kinds of cookies for him and the kids to eat. He worked our evening shift. The kids loved it when he was working. We would pick at him and tell him he spent more on cookies than he made.   Delia and Sonya were our Spanish employees and they would teach the kids how to sing and count in Spanish.

We lived in a good middle class neighborhood. Everyone was nice, and we knew almost everyone on the block so the kids could play when we went home. We had great neighbors who lived beside us, and across the road from us. Angie and Eddie who lived beside us were also great friends. They loved our kids, and we loved their two boys. They also went to the same church we went to.

We were growing in the business world so fast and doing great opening companies in other cities. A lot of times we had to go in two different directions to get companies up and running training managers in those offices. Life was exciting and we were always on the run not realizing we were setting ourselves for a great fall. I was by no means settled down. If things didn't go my way, I would load up and go back to Mississippi. We would run all the time till things would just explode. Just imagine split families, four kids, six companies, and we were in our early twenties. We were saved but didn't know the only way to make it as a child of God was to have a relationship with Him. He is your refuge! So in the mix of everything being so good there was a time bomb that we were not aware of. We did have life by the tail; it was good. Mom would say all the time ya'll need to be saving, putting money back. But not us because we were young having the time of our lives. About four years into our marriage we sold the house in the good neighborhood to buy and move to the country club house on the hill. It was beautiful with a privacy fence surrounding the back yard. We didn't have great neighbors. Sometimes people would speak, but for the most not. These were private folks, too busy.

I remember one Christmas Eve we had left home early that morning. I put on a load of sheets to wash because our parents were coming in for Christmas. I had a doctor's appointment two hours away so we were gone till late that evening. As we turned on our street water was coming down the road. The entire house was flooded, and Christmas presents were floating in the living room. The kitchen looked like a lake. The water was rippling in waves on the video camera. Our parents hadn't even seen our new house yet. What a surprise. Hampton had to go to the office on a bond call, and I was left with all that mess. I began to sweep cold water out the front door, and I heard the fire truck. I thought, Oh Lord it's on fire now. It wasn't on fire, but the fire department came out and carried all of our furniture out in the yard, swept the water out and did all they could to help. I was so surprised. I didn't know that they also helped in floods. When Hampton got to the office, someone had told him to call them and they would come out and help. In all this commotion our next door neighbor told Hampton that he had seen water coming out from under the garage when he left that morning. Oh well, he went on about his day taking care of his own business. It reminds me of the parable that Jesus told of the good Samaritan.

A certain man went down from Jerusalem to Jericho, and fell among thieves, who stripped him of his clothing, wounded him, and   departed, leaving him half dead. "Now by chance a certain priest came down that road. And when he saw him, he passed by on the other side. "Likewise a Levite, when he arrived at the place, came   and looked, and passed by on the other side. "But a certain   Samaritan, as he journeyed, came where he was. And when he saw him, he had compassion. "So he went to him and bandaged his wounds, pouring on oil and wine; and he set him on his own animal, brought him to an inn, and took care of him. "On the next day, when he departed, he took out two denarii, gave them to the innkeeper, and said to him, "Take care of him; and whatever more you spend, when I come again, I will repay you." "So which of these three do you think was neighbor to him who fell among the thieves?"

Jesus was talking to a certain lawyer who asked him a question thinking he was going to trick Jesus. But, as we see as always Jesus turns it back on them. We so quickly get our focus off of Jesus and onto ourselves and our needs. Do you see how our lives relate to Jesus' parable? But I do believe that if we had still been living in our old neighborhood they would have got in touch with us, or called the fire department themselves.

That Christmas was a lot of fun for the kids, because we stayed in a hotel which had an indoor heated pool and putt-putt golf. We had a lot of close family time. Soon mom and dad had to go back home, but we continued for over two weeks in the hotel. It had already gotten old by then to us all. I had even had a minor surgery, while locked up in that hotel room and the walls began to close in. When we got home we were so excited. We were back on our busy schedule. The kids were back in school, and we were always working. Hampton was always thinking of new ideas to promote the business. We had cut a couple of advertising spots on our local television station. We decided to do one with the jail house rock song playing in the back ground. I had made two outfits black and white stripes, and we had the ball and chain. It was so cute. We cut one with the girls (Jacqueline and Amanda). They were about five and seven years old. They were on a bed behind these bars doing the twist to the song. They were laughing so hard they were about to fall. It was such a cute commercial everybody loved it. We got a call from DHS telling us they better not see that commercial again because it was not fitting for a child, and we would see them in person next if it wasn't taken off the air. So of course we had it taken off the air. It was such a hit we decided to change the name of S and H bonding to Elvis bonding, but that didn't last long either. We got a call from Elvis's attorney in Memphis telling us we had twenty-four hours to get the name changed or else. Yes, we changed the name back to S and H bonding faster than we changed it the first time. We were always brainstorming to come up with new business plans. Some were good and some not so good!

We had the companies five to six years, and we began to talk about selling them and moving back to Mississippi. So in the summer of 1990 the girls Jacqueline, Amanda and I moved back. We bought a house and forty acres. It had to be totally remodeled before we could move in so my mom, girls and I began to tear walls down, carpet up, and totally gut the house. We finished by the time Hampton moved down. He stayed in Texas and sold the house and businesses. We were set for the next five years. It was a month to month pay out. We had great plans and had started a new business before we left that we could do in Mississippi. Within a few months our world fell upside down. Our new business wasn't going over in Mississippi's different atmosphere, and the sheriff came to our office and got all of our records. The new owner couldn't get his license so he wasn't able to pay us. So all the businesses were closed. We had to move back, but we never talked about that.

Detour
2

We were just turning in circles.
Everything that could go wrong was going
wrong. And we were now out of church, after
we moved home, we never looked for a
church home. We never knew of a
relationship with God. So we began to do
carpenter work on our house. My aunts
wanted us to do some little jobs, and some
weren't so little. But it seemed like always
when we finished the job we had gone in the
hole. So I got a job at our local hardware
store. I was so frustrated everything was
going wrong. Soon Hampton had also come
to work there. We began to talk about
opening a restaurant, grabbing at straws,
doing anything to give us back the life style
we had. (Of course we couldn't see all this
because we were in the storm). We found a
building and began to remodel it, and get it
set up and opened. Mother and I were
working around ninety hours a week. There
was a lot of frustration, a lot of work and the
business was still running in the red. The

girls were turning into teenagers, and Jacqueline was rebelling against me a lot because she wanted to know her real mother. I think she thought if she could get me to leave then maybe there would be a chance of her mom coming back. So the night I left it was really bad, and I had her to tell Hampton that she wanted me to leave. I know now she was the child that was hurting, and I ran away from her. She was pushing me away when really the one we love the most is the one we hurt the most. (Why is that?) I was not strong enough to handle all that coming at me. I just knew to run. That was the curse that my dad gave to me. He ran out on us and chose to live on the streets until he died. If we don't know God's Word, we don't have His wisdom to know curses and blessings are handed down. That was the straw that broke our marriage. The day I signed my divorce papers was the night that I had my encounter with God. That night I had a wreck that should have killed me, but I kept hearing this voice over and over "Be still don't move. You will be all right." So many people would see my vehicle and say God surely was with you, and I would reply, yes He was. But, I had head knowledge not heart knowledge. My heart had turned cold, and I never had a relationship with God or understood I could. So I just kept moving forward with my walls up and my heart cold. Hampton even came to the hospital as soon as he heard about the wreck. I was so cold to him. I was finished and moving on in my life. When things go wrong in our life, if we don't turn to Jesus Christ we end up making a bigger mess than the one we are in.

Then I totally walked away from God and turned to the party scene. I was going to the bar almost every night of the week finding more and more trouble. Satan likes you to think you're having the time of your life. I do remember that voice inside me. When I would wake up I felt all yucky inside and would think that's wrong, but by evening I would be drawn to the same old scene.

As far as work the restaurant wasn't making it, and mother and I couldn't keep up the hours we were doing and couldn't afford to hire someone, so we decided to close it. She got a job, and I decided to go to school so for the next eighteen months, I would carry Amanda to school and be on my way to Meridian to school myself. I went to Moore's Career College and received my diploma as a professional secretary. I already had the experience just not the education. I graduated with a 3.9 GPA the highest in the class. I would get home just in time for her to get off the school bus. The days I didn't go to school I cleaned houses to support us. After I graduated I got a job as a secretary and loved it. I worked there for a couple of years till I got married, and it became a problem with my marriage so I quit my job thinking that would help with my marriage. I knew all the time that it wasn't my job that was the problem, but I tried to make it work. Now I didn't just have Amanda. We had had a son, Austin, to raise and take care of. So shortly that marriage ended in abuse and alcohol. I had to find another job. I started waiting tables at a local restaurant.

Back On the Path
3

    I recall one day I was so tired and disgusted that I would venture back into the bonding business. It was a demanding job twenty- four seven, but that's what I liked best knowing that I was helping someone in a time of need. So I started checking out our local jail and talking to local judges and police officers and making my appearance at the jail. I opened an office downtown by the courthouse. To my surprise the business just started booming. I was getting calls day and night and a lot of the time I would have to carry Austin with me because Amanda would be gone. I would just put him on the back seat with a blanket and pillow and he would sleep until we would get back home. Then I would get him out and put him back to bed. Some nights we would go out more than once. But, that was my job, and we all made the best of it. (I was back on my journey but unaware of it!) Business was great, and I was back on my journey, but I still was drinking and partying and that wasn't in God's plan. When I was married, I always wanted a happy family with no drinking, but if I wasn't married I took on the party scene myself so guess what kind of men I attracted? Those like me - all messed up!

In my own sick way of thinking, I believed I could fix them if I would just love them more, when in truth I could not even fix myself. You would think I could have seen that in my life. (But I always heard stupid is as stupid does). I was stupid a lot!

When I was partying, and then feeling all yucky inside that feeling never left me. Years went by but that yucky feeling was always there the next morning to remind me this wasn't the life that God had planned for me.

I praise God that he never gave up on me and he won't give up on you. We never know when our time on this earth is up. We are only passing through. We are on our journey, an eternal one to heaven or to hell.

God Is In Control
_4_

(Praise God) One day I had a friend who wanted me to go to massage school with her. So we went to the school and checked it out. I enrolled, but she said she would later. I remember the first day the owner of the school saying no one is here by accident. That's the only thing I can recall about that first day of school because those words stuck with me. I knew when I started to school I wouldn't be able to drink and hang out with my friends like I did. And that I knew was good deep inside because I never raised Amanda to see me in the party world as I was raising Austin. And I didn't know how to get off the merry-go-round of life. I was really hurt inside and didn't want anyone to know it. (But of course everybody knew it but me)

Massage school was a two year program so I would work in the bonding business all day and go to school four nights a week. I would drive back and forth one hundred and eight miles a night. Before I graduated I was tired of the drive back and forth. I was also glad that my life was changing before the end of the two years. I had already opened up a day spa keeping me occupied six days a week. Then (isn't it cool how God works everything out) my son was around five years old, and one day out of the blue, he said "Mommy I want to go to church." I had no idea where that came from because we didn't hang out with church people. But, later I asked him if he got this from his friends at school. He said, "No, I just wanted to go." Now that was the Holy Spirit working in a child's heart because we didn't listen to church on television, read the Bible, or listen to Christian music, or even talk about going to church. But when it's time to come home to the Father, the Holy Spirit will draw you.

No one can come to Me unless the Father who sent Me draws him; and I will raise him up at the last day. (John 6:44)

So that weekend we went shopping for some church clothes. I thought about what church I wanted to go to. We went to one in our neighborhood. That first Sunday I felt so judged, but I'm not sure that anyone even knew we were there. Then that week one guy friend (Mr. Pete) heard that we had come to church that Sunday and invited us to Sunday school. He told me he would be looking for us in the parking lot and show us where our classes were. And that following Sunday we went, and he was outside waiting to walk us to our classes just like he had promised. That always meant so much to me. I never felt like that was where I was to be, but I never forgot the kindness that he showed us. He took a special place in my heart that day. I had seen a lot of church people in my life before, but that day I saw a Christian. Mr. Pete was a man who had Jesus living in him, and he didn't care what others might think. I was a single woman living at the well that day. Mr. Pete allowed Jesus to live in him.

A woman of Samaria (sinner) came to draw water. Jesus said to her, "Give me a drink." For his disciples had gone away into the city to buy food. Then the woman of Samaria (sinner) said to Him. "How is it that You, being a Jew, ask a drink from me, a Samaritan woman?" For Jews (church people) have no dealings with Samaritans.(sinners)

This Samarian woman thought that Jesus was like all the Jews. Sometimes we think just like she did. Was it her fault or had she been already judged so many times that she judged the one and only Jesus Christ? That Sunday I didn't understand at that time that there are church people and there are Christians. Thank God that day I saw the difference between the two. Anyone can go to church, but to be a Christian you have to show the love of Christ in you for others, no matter what others might think. That day Mr. Pete walked it out for me to see the love of Christ. I thank God that he allowed Jesus to shine through him.

We went to church there for several months when Austin decided that he wanted to be baptized and was not going to wait another Sunday. He wanted to go down and make a confession of faith. So at that moment in my life I knew if he went down, I had to go down and really change my life style. I still did not understand how Jesus comes in and does the cleaning. So we did, and that night we were going to another church to hear my friend sing. That was the night that Jesus met me right where I was and drew me into His wonderful presence at the altar. I did not want to leave. I wanted to stay there in that presence with Him. I was still so unaware of how our Father works.   When His spirit comes in, He never leaves us. He is with us wherever we go and whatever we do. It is   so amazing how He puts new friends in your life at that very moment. He gives us all we need, but it's our choice if we walk it out or try to hang on to our old friends too.   Nothing is wrong with them. They just don't see life as you do anymore.

They stumble, being disobedient to the word, to which they also were appointed. But you are a chosen generation a royal priesthood, a holy nation, His own special people, that you may proclaim the praises of him who called you out of darkness into His marvelous light; who once were not a people but are now the people of God, who had not obtained mercy but now have obtained mercy.

Peter 2:8-10

We are special people set apart from the ways of this world.

God's Love
5

God is so much greater than our earthly parents and wants so much more for us. He has unconditional love for us and wants us to have it for others. We need the love of Christ who died on the cross to bear our sins because He loved us first. If we could just get that and grab hold of it, we could change the world because He lives in us and desires us to have the heart He had for the lost. He didn't care if they were dirty, clean, pretty, ugly, skinny, fat, rich, poor, black, white, purple or green. He saw the breath of the creator in each one of us. My prayer as you read this book is that you would also have the love of Christ in you and desire to get on the journey that He has called to you. If you have not accepted Christ as your personal savior and Lord of your life, I pray that you would stop right here and invite Him into your heart.

Lord Jesus, I believe that you died for me and rose from the dead and are sitting on the right hand of the Father. Jesus, I ask you to come into my heart and forgive me of my sins. I want you to be Master and Lord over my life from this day forward. I love you in Jesus name. Amen, and Amen.

It's just that easy. All you have to do it say it, and believe….

As I began to walk out the journey that God had planned in my life, my eyes were open to the spirit world, the supernatural. Remember it's a journey. We think we are saved, and we know everything. But not so, we haven't even learned to walk.

As newborn babes, desire the pure milk of the word, that you may grow thereby, if indeed you have tasted that the Lord is gracious.   *1 Peter 2:2, 3*

We have to start growing that spirit man that lives inside of us. How? By reading His word, spending time praying, talking to God, listening, and having fellowship with other believers. Listening is most important.

I didn't have anybody to explain this to me, and I surely didn't read a book to figure it out. I was on fire, and I wanted to be involved in anything and everything at the church. So it wasn't long at all until my world was turned upside down.

Do not be overcome by evil, but overcome evil with good.

Romans 12:21

My mother went into the hospital to have a minor surgery and died from complications from the surgery. So much went wrong, but all I could do was cry and pray. As I began to seek His face, He began to give me visions of writing, and I began to wrestle with it knowing nobody knew my past and some of it was so horrible I had blocked it out.   I surely didn't want to reopen it in my mind let alone write a book about it. So for ten months I was praying for answers, and He was coming to me in visions working all my prayers out and giving me directions to write, speak, and from the book royalties would be a shelter for women. That was over nine years ago. It hasn't all come to pass, but I know it will. I have had so many detours in my journey, but from each one He has given me another book to write.

But as I wrote that first book (<u>You Are My Child</u>), he began to heal deep wounds inside of me. He told me in the visions He would bless me, and that He has truly done. He has healed me. So many people read my book, and say I'm so sorry.   I tell them all, that's all garbage. That's my testimony and the point is how He carried me through the storm. I've never been on nerve medicine or drugs to hide my pain of my past. I look back now and know that He had His hand on me all the time.

This is my third book that He has allowed me to write and given me the desire to write. I still have to be honest. I love the feeling of His presence when I'm writing, but I still so wrestle with it because it is so hard for me. I am horrible in English and always have been. I write as I talk just plain and simple. I guess I want to be all that and a bag of chips... But He made me plain, and simple and I thank God I can never get the big head and think I did this. Because it's not me, it's God putting it all together. I can look back and read it and stay humble before His throne. Thank you, Father, for never giving up on me, and I truly ask for your forgiveness for wrestling with writing so much. To write, I have to be still. That in itself is a God task.

So as I continue on this journey of mine, I began to speak at different churches and places. After about a year my old church started having problems, and my family and I and several other families moved to other churches. That is when I started visiting All Seasons Worship Center and soon after became a member, and now we have been there little over eight years.

Not long after my first book was published I began to seek ways to get this shelter that God has placed in my spirit. Every avenue that I tried seemed to be a dead end. I would keep pushing. But finally after a lot of tears and hard work and board meetings, auctions, conferences and thrift stores, I can see it's just not the right time. But I know in my spirit it is to come!

One day in all my tears and confusion I was at work and got a phone call asking to speak to Krista the other massage therapist, and I said she's not here. So the caller said, "You do massage right?" I told her yes, and set up her appointment. She came in the next hour, or so. Her name was Sandra, and she was sent to me from God. I began to give her massage, and she leaned up and said, "God sent me" and from that day we have been sisters. Our first trip was the next day. We went to visit a shelter. On her heart was a drug and rehab shelter and in mine was domestic shelter. We got there that day and the night before the drug rehab had burned down and right beside it was a domestic shelter. So we got to talk and visit with all of them. That was my third shelter to go to. I had visited another one outside of Memphis and went to a homeless shelter in Jackson. God was showing me these places even though the money sources were not forming.

A few weeks after that we visited a recovery center outside of Chunky. And a few months later a friend and I spoke at a recovery center in Jackson. I just know every time I go to one of these places I'm just amazed that I feel at home, and my mind starts running how, when. God, I know where, but how is it going to all come to pass? By Faith!

Faith is the substance of things hoped for but the evidence of things not yet seen.

Hebrews 11:1

I finally know it's in God's timing, not Wanda's. Right now it's time for me to continue to write and focus on raising my son.

Stinking Thinking

6

As mine and Sandra's friendship grew, we were always going somewhere and meeting God's people. So on one trip she got in touch with hand maidens where she got her minister's license. I went with her and two other young ladies out to New Boston, TX.

Sandra thought they would open up to me on their way out there. **_I'm thinking;_** I may be able to help someone. Right, God has such a since of humor. I think I may be able to help her, and as soon as we walked into the house of MS Nancy the president of hand maidens and now Servant hood Ministries, she introduced herself to me, and
Said, "Wanda, tell me a little about you." Out of my mouth came
"Well, I'm Wanda Nance, and this weekend I'm supposed to get married."
She said, "Supposed to!"
I quickly reframed my words. I mean this

weekend I'm getting married. She has such a loving smile one like I never had seen.

She said, "We'll see." I thought I came to help someone else, and now she is doing a counseling meeting with me. These meetings were not like I was going in to tell her my problems and have her give me advice. We would go in and open up with prayer just me and her, and she would invite the Holy Spirit in to talk to me. But I couldn't hear Him so we would go back in my life and invite him in all the way back to my childhood. The Holy Spirit carried me back and showed me that I always end up doing something that I didn't really want to do in the first place. But I would say yes rather than hurt someone's feelings. And I had carried that way of thinking into my adulthood where I would end up hurting someone later rather than being honest at first. The man I was to marry and I both knew inside that we had a lot of adjusting going on but I kept thinking, and everybody kept telling me we were perfect together. Part of me felt that way and part of me didn't, but I was headed into a one way street with my feeling going two ways. He could see that in me and didn't know how to stop it either. I remember after that first session with Ms. Nancy I felt like a ton of bricks was removed, and I knew I had to call off the wedding. That night I didn't sleep much for thinking how I could do this. We were both very involved with our church. It was going to be a simple but big church wedding. My mind was racing a hundred miles an hour. How was I going to tell him! I needed to cancel the cake and all the decorations I had rented. But I was also at such peace. The next morning Sandra got up before me and was out on the front porch swing. I went out there and she asked, "How I was. Did I get any rest?" I said, "Finally." I will never forget we sat on the porch and watched this squirrel run across a power line, down a tree and back up. Everywhere he went this bird was right behind him pecking him, and he was steadily running. We watched this for it seemed like forever.

Then the Holy Spirit spoke to Sandra and said that's the way Satan does in our lives. He is always running behind us pecking right on our tail. If we keep moving like the squirrel, he can only peck behind us.

So Ms. Nancy came out to join us, and she and Sandra went to the office to have her session. I continue to sit on the porch that morning reading my Bible and talking with God. His word came to life to me that morning.

Finally, my brethren, be strong in the Lord and in the power of His might. Put on the whole armor of God, that you may be able to stand against the wiles of the devil. For we do not wrestle against flesh and blood, but against principalities, against powers, against the rulers of the darkness of this age, against spiritual hosts of wickedness in the heavenly places. Therefore take up the whole armor of God, that you may be able to withstand in the evil day, and having done all, to stand. Stand therefore, having girded your waist with truth, having put on the breastplate of righteousness, and having shod your feet with the preparation of the gospel of peace, above all, taking the shield of faith with which you will be able to quench all the fiery darts of the wicked one. And take the helmet of salvation, and the sword of the Spirit, being watchful to this end with all perseverance and supplication for all the saints and for me, that utterance may be given to me, that I may open my mouth boldly to make known the mystery of the gospel, for which I am an ambassador in chains: that in it I may speak boldly, as I ought to speak.
Ephesians 6:10-20

As I read those scripture and sat there I felt so free and at peace. I knew that I had to take a stand. Did that make life easy? Not at all. I had to go back, talk to Kenneth, call the wedding off, and of course we broke up. I was the big bad wolf in the church for a long time. Maybe not to my face but to my back. But God had given me peace and a new direction to walk through the valley. Sandra and Nancy came back shortly.

Sandra said, "I'm going to retake some of these Bible studies, I've got my license but would you like to take them with me." Then we can go together. The book and class is seventy-five dollars every three months.

The Lord had already put that in my spirit to get my license, so I quickly said yes. Several months before that it was in my spirit to get my license, and I had talked to my pastor's wife, and I knew that there was no way with the denomination I was with because I had been divorced. So as I sat there that morning I knew in my spirit that this was a God ordained week. I was so excited, but I also knew I had to STAND.

So the next two years of my life I was going back and forth to Texas, and I ended up taking a counseling class also. Sometimes with the Bible study, counseling class and conferences I was going every month. I loved it. I would get such a spiritual high, and all the people truly loved me. They knew I wasn't perfect, and it was okay. There was so much agape love that flowed out of Ms. Nancy, to every one of us. It was always a life changing weekend. God knew I needed that with all the emotions going on in my church. I surely wanted to leave, but God would not release me to leave. All I could hear was a sermon that Pastor had preached that if you left one church to come here running from your problems, and you leave it will only be worse. I would think I can't stand it if it gets any worse. So I would stay another week and another week until it seemed to get better.

Now, a few years have passed since that moment in my journey, and actually

Kenneth and I get along well. He knows where I stand and I know where he stands, and we are able to be great friends. If I really need somebody to talk to who can set me straight, Kenneth is one of them. He doesn't care if he hurts my feelings or not, he going to tell me like it is. And I pretty much do for him the same. We are real with each other. We have a special friendship and great respect for each other.

This is Kenneth's testimony. He has given me permission to write it in hopes it will help someone else. We are overcomers by the blood of the Lamb and the words of our testimony. I am proud of where God has brought him from and to.

My testimony is very simple but rare. I was a Methamphetamine addict from 1992 - till September 2003.

I was a methamphetamine addict crack, cocaine, and cigarettes. I smoked for twenty-five years. My testimony is a lot like the normal, lost everything done very little jail time but somewhat rare. Because after smoking three hundred dollars of crack one night. I went through the normal talking down to myself. When are you ever going to catch on? You've lost everything and everybody, except some of my children. There was a voice now I know that was the voice of God that said, "If you go back to the drugs you not coming back." I took Him for His word. I came to the church God drew me too. (John 6:44)

God saved me and delivered me from all those years of misery. But here what makes it rare. I've never had a desire for the drugs since. I went cold turkey! But here is where I'm different from most I am Free!

God delivered me so I have a choice to go back now. But I chose not to hang with my old

so called friends. I'm quick to say, "NO!"
That's the key when someone says let's go
hang out. I'm quick to say, No!!!!
I can't toy with my gift God gave me. Before
long those people will go away. You will have
new friends that are on your side.
But most of all you will have the spirit of God
living in you. Jesus as your Lord. I take God
at His word, if I go back there's no coming
back. Going back is not an option!
                                   Kenneth

Open Door
7

Rehab was a woman who saw an open door and quickly stepped through it. She didn't think about treason and helping the enemy.

When her king asked her to bring out the spies who had been seen entering her inn, she said, "Yes, the men came to me, but I did not know where they were from. And it happened as the gate was being shut, when it was dark that the men went out. Where they went I do not know; pursue them quickly, for you may overtake them."
Joshua
_2:4-5_

Rehab had heard about God. She chose to acknowledge and trust God. She helped the spies which was God's chosen people and from her hiding them in her home, till they could escape safely. She had them to promise that they would not destroy her and her family.

The Bible states, *"And Joshua spared Rehab the harlot, her father's household, and all that she had. So she dwells in Israel to this day, because she hid the messengers whom Joshua sent to spy out Jericho."*
Joshua 6:26

Rehab is also mentioned in Matthew's list of Jesus Christ ancestors. There was an open door that she didn't question. She just quickly obeyed. And from her obedience she went from a prostitute to a child of God...

On my first Bible study class weekend, Sandra called and told me she wasn't going to be able to go. Everything in my mind said, "Don't go. You don't know any of those people out there." Then I quickly thought Lord you opened that door for me, and I'm going. I have to admit I was a little frustrated with Sandra. I got there and had a wonderful weekend. And on my trip back home I heard the Holy Spirit say "I wanted to know if you would go all by yourself." So I knew then this journey was meant for me and God alone. We had some wonderful trips back and forth in those six hours of driving. Sandra did take the counseling class with me, but she never went on any of the Bible study weekends.

And I was okay with that because I knew it was my journey. She had already taken hers.

After that first weekend of going you would think all the others would have come easy. But I remember one time I went, and I was so short of money that I fixed snacks to eat. When I got out there, they had changed the weekend and forget to tell me. I got to the church and no one was there. I went to Ms. Nancy's house and no one was there. I called Sandra, my mentor in Texas. There was no answer, but soon she called me back. I was already at the hotel so she told me; she wanted to meet me for brunch the next morning before I left. So we met and went to Old Charley in Texarkana and then came back to the church. Before I left she said, "The Lord told me to give this to you." She handed me ten dollars. Only the Lord knew I had to have ten dollars more for gas to make it home. If it had been more money I wouldn't thought so much about it, but it was exactly what I had to have to make it home. God is good! Will He test our Faith? You'd better believe He will. He wants to know that He can trust you. But He will never fail you.

He is always there. He knows the money that's in your wallet because I didn't know exactly how much I had. I knew I was close, but the feeling I got when she gave me that ten dollars made me feel so much better than a hundred dollars would have because I knew Sandra heard to the penny what God said. And I knew my Daddy knew everything about me. And God so wants us to trust everything to him.

Then the day finally came for us to graduate and get our license. It was at our fall convention, and Sandra went with me. My Pastor and first lady also came to celebrate with me. We broke for lunch that day and the four of us went out to eat and then went shopping at antique shop. We had so much fun. That was their favorite kind of shop to go to, and New Boston just happened to have a great one. They stayed for the ceremony, and Pastor prayed over me. After they left, I had several people come up to me and tell me what compassion my pastor had, and what an awesome man of God he is. I told them I am so honored to be under his leadership.

Sandra and I stayed for the rest of the convention and then we drove back home, so we could be at our church on Sunday morning.

<u>Love My People</u>
8

*So when they had eaten breakfast,
Jesus said to Simon Peter, "Simon, son of
Jonah, do you love me more than these?" He
said to Him, "Yes Lord; You know that I love
You." Jesus said, "Feed My lambs."*

*John
21:15*

As we read this we know that Jesus
repeats Himself to Simon Peter three times.
That was letting Peter know how important it
was to him to carry out His word to the whole
world.
Peter was quick to follow Jesus, quick to
speak before he thought. Jesus trusted Peter
over the other ten disciples. Peter was quick
to step out of the boat and walk on water
while the others stayed in, afraid of
drowning. Jesus knew that Peter would curse
and deny Him before the next morning. Jesus
also knew that Satan had asked to sift Peter as
sand. Not the other eleven, the one that was

quick to respond. The one that Jesus at the end could trust to turn His ministry over to.

Several months after I was licensed I just began to pray for God to give me his agape love. Really didn't know why I was praying this, but it was so in my spirit. As I would go to the jail to bond someone out, I would always try to tell them about Jesus. I never went in head strong. I learned to listen to the spirit because if God wasn't leading me then they surely weren't going to listen. But, I continued to pray for several months for His agape love in me.

Then one day I was at the jail looking at docket book bonding someone out. When one of the lady jailors, Angela, came out and asked me, "Wanda, you got your license. Would you be interested in ministering to the ladies here? They don't have anybody, and the men have several people that come." I said, "Sure who do I need to talk to?" She told me to get in contact with Chief Carson, so I did. I began that next Thursday night ministering with the ladies, and that moment I knew why I had been praying for his agape love. He has so given that to me. I so love these women, and when I go there it doesn't matter to me who they are, or what they are charged with, or where they came from. I want to tell them about Jesus and where He can take them and the love and peace that only he can give. No man, no woman, no money, no drugs, no things can do that - only Jesus!!!

I remember the first time I went in. We met outside in the yard. There were twelve girls, and an officer stayed out there with us. I never go in with this attitude that I'm better, I just was never caught. I told them my testimony and left them my book to read and pass around.   When I closed that night I asked if anyone wanted me to pray for them, and this one girl said yes, and as we began to pray. Every one of the girls began to pray with us. It was so awesome, and I was so touched by the power of God.   That one girl she touched my heart. She had a hard life and not much education. She was what we would call slowly, and from that she had been used by people to get their way with her, and this one guy had talked her into signing these checks so she was in jail, and he had the money. She had such a spirit of lust on her. She knew it, but it controlled her. She would stand at the men's door all night, and talk trash with these guys. She would ask me to pray for her, but she wouldn't stay away from that door. She so needed somebody to love her. She had no one. Her mother wouldn't come visit her, and she didn't have a dad. She remembered her sister being burned in a house fire when she was a baby. She would study and read the word, but that evil spirit had her in bondage. I prayed when she went on to prison that she would be set completely free. I hope one day to meet her again. She is special to me, and I still have the letters she wrote me while in Scott county jail.

The next couple of times we met outside, and then the time changed and it was dark, and I couldn't see to read. So we started staying in the cell.

At the very beginning of my ministry I met two young ladies that broke my heart. They were prostitutes; they both sold their bodies for drugs. One was twenty-four at the time that I first met her. She was beautiful. She could draw, sing and had such a sweet personality. I will never forget when I got the chance to lead her to the Lord, we were outside on the yard and I walked back to the cell with them. She just stood at the door and hung on me saying I feel so warm and peaceful inside. I feel clean! When she got out she did for a couple of weeks come and go to church with me. Then it was excuse calls till no calls at all. Soon she was right back out there, worse than before. She would get in and out of the jail till the last time I saw her she was in court on her way to prison with full blown aids. Satan is out to kill, steal and destroy!

The other young lady was twenty-seven and also beautiful. I'm not sure how much talent she had. She was reserved. She had been on the streets since she was eleven. Her childhood was stolen from her and she never knew a different life. She would get in jail and stay for weeks. I remember one time I was in court with her and she told the judge as soon as I get out I'm going to church with Ms. Sissy (my nickname) I'm changing my life. Judge told her that was good and he was glad to hear that. That same afternoon I was writing a bond and she went to the restroom and snuck right by me and out the door she went. She was back into the only world she knew. It broke my heart. I could see the good in her but couldn't reach her. As she would come in and out of the jail after that time, she would curl up into a ball on the floor and try not to listen but the Holy Spirit was still drawing her. I have had numerous people to call me asking me if I knew that tall blonde lady that walks the street. I would say yes and just pray for her. God has a plan for her because He burdens so many people's hearts about her. The other day I went to the jail and heard that they had a missing person call and I found out it was her. It broke my heart. She has been missing for a few weeks now. They figure they will find her in a ditch or creek somewhere. Satan is out to kill, steal and destroy!

One Thursday I came to look at the jail docket when one of the other bond persons said I couldn't get a certain lady out, and anybody who does is a sorry person to. I can't believe anybody would kill their own baby. I didn't say anything but I quickly left, thinking I don't want to hear that and go in with a judging spirit about this lady. I prayed about it because I surely didn't want the heart of man I had to have the heart of God. That night as I ministered to the girls there were a few new ones, but I didn't know which one she was. After I left I found out she was sitting right beside me, and I'm so thankful to God that I had his agape love, and it didn't matter where or who she was. God so loved her that Jesus died for her, as he did for you, and as he did for me. I tried so hard to reach her, but I never could. At one time I thought she was coming around, and then she got out of jail, but when she returned several months later she wouldn't even listen to the Bible studies. Her heart was hard.

The week after that mother had been arrested for murdering her child, the grandmother and aunt were in there. They were charged with capital murder also. That night after Bible studies both ladies gave their lives to the Lord. I watched them grow in the Lord. I would go in, and they would be on the news. They were on national news for several weeks. They would ask if I had seen it. I told them I didn't watch that. And we began to grow as sisters in Christ. They were in the county jail about ten months. We would pray and see doors open, and then doors closed in their case. I remember the night before they went to court the next morning. They had signed a guilty plea because they were scared and looking at the death penalty. I told them I wanted them to get in their quiet time with God and do what He said do. Do it! That next day I was sitting in court listening to their guilty plea, and it broke my heart because something in my spirit told me that wasn't what God told them to do. Months later I got to visit the aunt in prison, and I asked her what God told you to do. She said not to take the guilty plea, but the lawyers said it was too late......

"And do not fear those who kill the body but cannot kill the soul. But rather fear Him who is able to destroy both soul and body in hell."
Matthew 10:28

This is the aunt's testimony. She has given me permission to write it in my book.

11-24-09

My name is Stephanie Bell, and here is my testimony. First of all. I want to thank God for being able to share this with you. I want to praise God for giving me strength, and the knowledge to say no to drugs. I've never done drugs, or been abused by my parents. But on November 9, 2008. I lost my 4 year old nephew (Austin). Then when I didn't think things could get no worse my mom, and I were arrested November 12, 2008, and charged for his death. My 4 year old son (Cortney), my 6 year old nephew (Bubba), and my 8 year old niece (Erin) were all placed with DHS that same day. And it's been a year since I've seen them. Then on December 29, 2008 my grandmother (my mom's mother) passed away. And on September 29, 2009 my mom and I took a plea, and was sentenced to life without parole. On October 1, 2009, we were sent to MDOC during all this time all our family, and so called friends turned on us. This would have been a terrible year for some people, but during all my losing love ones. I was able to find my Heavenly Father. I got saved November 9, 2008 as well as my mom. On November 24, 2008, we were baptized. My Father has healed my foot, and my stomach. He gave me strength to deal with all that happened. If it had not been for losing my loved ones I'd still be doing the devils work. Losing them was my wake up call. Although I'm in prison for this I didn't do. It's ok, cause I know one thing my Father has a plan, and purpose for my being here, and once I've done his work I know I'll Lord for a year now, and it's the best feeling be set free. I have been walking with the ever. As each day passes I hunger for more of his word. I thank God for being a forgiving, and loving Father. For giving me a chance, and saving my soul from hell, so I can have eternal life with him. Yes I lost everything I owned, and everyone I loved in that year, but I gained eternal life with God! Amen. I also want to give a very special thanks to Sister Wanda Nance for being here for me, and teaching me God's word, and for her love, and encouragement. If not for her I would have gave up more than once because I didn't think I could take no more, but she didn't let me. She reminded me of God's great love, and that his word says he'll never leave nor forsake thee. Nor will he put more on me than I can take. So instead of giving up she taught

me to go to God with my problems. That's what I did, and now I am stronger, and when I have problems are feel alone I turn to Him losing everything was a stepping stone for me.
I give all glory, and power to God… Amen and Amen.

Those are Stephanie's words, and she is still in prison at this time. But God is so good and using her so much. She got her GED and she is tutoring other ladies to get their GED, She is in Kairos (a Bible ministry). I no longer can go visit her since I started prison ministry at MDOC in Pearl. I know in my heart God is opening doors for me to be able to minister there. I feel in my spirit that's another part of my journey. I will discuss more as I walk out my journey of life. Where has God got you, or you on your journey. Are you wandering in the wilderness?

For the next two and a half years I would go to the jail and minister sometimes twice a week. At first I would go for hour, then it continued to get longer and longer. I enjoyed the girls so much and think they really do enjoy the time of Bible study that they don't have to worry about someone judging them. They can be real!

The most amazing thing I have seen is God always seems to have one that we call the spiritual mom and when she leaves, He will raise up another. He loves all of his children so much he doesn't want to see any go astray.

It has been so rewarding to me that God would use me. I have been able to lead several to the Lord and baptize them right in the shower. Yes I get wet too but that is great. I remember the first time I did this. I walked out of the cell that night wet and carrying my shoes. The officer looked at me real funny. I laughed and said I have been baptizing in the shower.

He said, "Oh ok!" We get real in there, and they know I love them, and I know they love me. And, the greatest thing is when I see them fall in love with Jesus. Some may leave and go back to their ways, but that seed is planted, and God does the watering and the increase. Sometimes they come right back in, and I tell them if they don't straighten up they will be back.

One girl they had locked in a cell by herself because she was HIV positive. I began to tell them to let me go in there too so I would go in with the group then I would go and share the word with her. She was so ashamed. I began to love her and tell her that Jesus had a plan for her. He wanted her to take a stand and minister to people that are just like her. I told her while she was in there to use that whole cell for preaching and to walk back and forth telling her testimony and ministering God's love in that cell. Practice it girl!

How many know that we are overcomers by the blood of the Lamb and the word of our testimony? What makes us strong is the word in us and being a light to the dark world.

I even got the chance to baptize her. I don't know how many I've gotten to lead to the Lord and baptize in there. I have never kept a record. Jesus is doing that.

My friend, a sister in Christ, started coming to the jail with me. She has such anointing on her. I love to just watch the Lord work through her. Sometimes I have to repent from envy. I think, I wish I had that anointing Lord when I know I can. It's called sacrifice spending and obeying God and watching Him grow in us.

This is Linda's testimony I asked her if she would write hers and give it to me to go in my book.

Jeremiah 12:5 "So, Jeremiah, if you are worn out in this footrace with men, what makes you think you can run against the horses?"

My name is Lynda and the above verse describes my journey with the Lord Jesus Christ. Everyday seems like a glorious but exhausting footrace. The love of the Lord and His love for humanity keeps me in the race.

I did not surrender my life to the Lord until the age of thirty-five during my fifth marriage. My mom filled the first seventeen years of my life with church where I learned about the Law of God, and the importance of not breaking it. To the despair of my parents and others who had great hopes for my life, I got pregnant at seventeen, my senior year. Now I not only knew the Law of God, but I also knew I could not live up to its requirements. The shame was not in being pregnant but the fact of everyone knew about my sin.

The shame of my revealed sin set into motion a tornado that would twist and spin for the next eighteen years. A tailspin of partying, one night stands, failed relationships, five marriages, and many thoughts of suicide swirled around and aftermath. I found my only hope in my around. Unbearable guilt and shame were its two beautiful children, and the snippets of Jesus I saw in other people.

*At the age of Thirty-five, I finally met the man Him, the man I heard about all my life, Jesus! He commanded that tornado of shame to be still. He loved me just for being me! November 6, 2002, I met Jesus and **nothing** has been the same since.*

Now I am forty-five and He is more wonderful than the day we met. He has taken all the mistakes and turned them into weapons of warfare. Every day is a new adventure. Because of Him, I am still married to my fifth husband, and I have found a Hope that can withstand any storm life can brew. He has grafted me into His most perfect vine to be a tool in the advancing of His kingdom. What a wonderful Father He is! In return I want my life to reflect Jesus. My favorite quote is one of D.L. Moody. It goes something like this, "The world has yet to see what can be done through one person who is totally committed to Christ." My ultimate goal is to one day "run against the horses."

Linda hadn't been going in with me long until we had a Jehovah's Witness lady in jail and full of the evil spirit. Then they started getting visits from a Jehovah's Witness person. They had the girls so confused. Every time we would go in they would ask questions and then look at her. She always was quiet and would pray with us. But she had no hope and didn't believe in Jesus. One time we went in there and another one of my girls, Crystal, was from my home town. She was young, beautiful, married and had kids but was bound by Satan and his biggest demon, drugs. She wanted to be set free and when she was in jail she was safe and loved the Lord with all of her heart. Crystal even got into a fight with this Jehovah's Witness lady that was twice her size. She would have choked Crystal to death if it hadn't been for the other ladies calling for help and trying to get her off of her. Crystal fought for the Lord Jesus Christ for whom she believed in. She still had the marks on her face when she died several months later after she had gone on to prison and they placed her on house arrest. I'm not sure what happened to her. I just know her son found her in the bed dead. But one thing I'm sure of - she loved the Lord!

There was another lady in jail who

came in soon after Stephanie and her mom went on to prison. From day one she had such a sweet spirit on her. She stayed in the word. I called her the spiritual mother. All the girls would come to her and want her to pray for them. They knew she was real because they watched her day after day. She stayed in the county about a year. The week before her court date came up she wanted me to baptize her. She wanted it all under the blood, but she knew that wouldn't change her circumstance. She was charged with murdering her husband. She went to court that week and took her guilty plea and went on to prison for fifteen years. It broke mine and Linda's heart because we knew in the spirit that there were more to it, but she didn't have the money to hire a lawyer to fight her case. So as we see this happen time and time again. These court appointed cases pushed under the rug... I could tell you case after case I have watched through the years. It breaks my heart!

I remember one girl who didn't weigh 100 lbs. and was very slow. She had gotten twenty years for statuary rape on a fourteen-year-old boy that weighed over two hundred pounds. And as I said she wasn't completely mentally right. When I first met her she would cry and ask me to pray for her that they would find out the truth. Later I found out what she was charged with and I couldn't believe it. But the law reads we are innocent until proven guilty but that's not how it works most of the time. If they don't have the money to fight the case then they don't have a chance most of the time.

This old world today is about money, power and greed.

Be My Servant
_9_

One Wednesday night I was at church service, and we always break up into small groups to pray before service. So in our group there were a couple of new ladies. I introduced myself, and we went around the circle for prayer requests. We finished praying, and the lady that was standing next to me asked, "What is your last name?" I told her, and she asked are you a bonds person. I said yes, and she told me I had gotten her out of jail and then put her back in jail. At that time I could have crawled under the chair. I told her I was sorry, and she said that was the best thing that had happened to her. Then she began to tell me that she had been indicted and had been out of state to see her boyfriend. But I came to talk to her at the visiting booth and gave her my book to read. As she was telling me all this, my eyes were filling with tears. I was so blessed, so overwhelmed and so grateful that God would use me and then share it all back to me a few years later when I needed to be encouraged to keep writing and ministering. When we have no idea that we are making a difference, God is making a difference. He is such a loving God! All this was flooding through my head…

At this time I hadn't started doing jail ministry. And didn't recall this at all, so I know that it was totally God working. I went home from church and pulled her file. I remembered her then. God had truly transformed this lady. I pulled her picture out of the file to give to her so she could truly see where God had brought her from.
This is her testimony…

I am 36 years old, I have 3 beautiful children, and I recently married a wonderful man.

But life was not all that great for me not so long ago. I was addicted to crystal meth. for 13 years. Over those years I ruined my life, and even worse- the lives of the people who loved me most. I would stay high for days, weeks, and to be honest, I stayed high every day for several years. I mean there was not a day that I did not use! I would try to hide it, and thought that I was doing a good job of it, but now I see that I really wasn't. I would steal from people who loved me-my parents, my friends, and worst of all I stole from my own kids. I not only stole from my children, but I did meth with them in the same house as me. I even took them with me when I would go get more drugs. I never thought of my children for one second. All I thought about was getting my drug.

I often ask myself why I started using. I had things that happened to me when I was little that I carried around for so long that I did not know how to deal with them. I just did not like who I was. I did not want to feel anything at all, I just wanted to be numb- and that is what I did for so many years.

I started getting into trouble with the law in 2004, but I refused to learn my lesson. Oh, I would say that I was trying, and I guess in my sick way of thinking, I did try for a little bit. But I never could quit using. Well, it finally happened. While I was working at Wal-Mart, I ended up stealing money from work. I was caught red-handed and was arrested in 2006 on felony embezzlement charges.

I was sitting in my county cell wondering how I screwed up my life so badly-and not just my life, but my kids' lives and all my family's lives as well. I used people, and hurt people, and started looking at the person that I had become, and I hated that person. It hurt so

bad to see what I had done to everyone. I would read my Bible while I was in the county jail, and pray, but I just never really realized what God had in store for me, until I got to the state penitentiary at Rankin county. I was sentenced to 3 years at MDOC, and I was scared to death! I cried, and prayed, but I know now that it was the kind of prayer you pray when you get into trouble, and just want out. It wasn't until I had been in state prison for several weeks, before I realized that God had a plan for me. I attended church service in prison, and do you know, for the first time since I was a kid, I really did learn something about God, and the Holy Spirit. I was raised up in church with good Christian parents, and I knew about God, and Jesus, and the Holy Spirit. But I never really understood what the Holy Spirit could do in my life. One night at church, it all of a sudden hit me who the Holy Spirit was, and I understood Him for the first time in my life. I cannot explain the feeling that came over me that night, but from that point on I knew that I was going to change. I went to every church service, and started reading my Bible, and doing every Bible study I could. I ended up being the one in charge of setting up for the church services, and running the sound system at all the services...
Within the next 6 months, I knew that I was

going to be okay. I learned that God had not turned his back on me-that I had turned my back on Him, and all I had to do was turn back to Him, and He would accept me with open arms. So that is just what I did. I asked God to forgive me, and to help me overcome my addiction, and the pain I had caused.

I know that He has forgiven me, and I am trying my best now to do what I can to make up for the things I did wrong. I cannot change the past, but I can change my future, and where I spend eternity. I have been given a second chance at life. And I am enjoying each and every day with my wonderful family.

You should have seen my excitement the first time I ran into my "old friends," and told them I did not go there anymore, and to stay away from me. I have been clean for 2 years, and 3 months, and could not have beat my demons if, God had not put me in a place where I was forced to get sober, and where I did not have a choice, but to sit down, and be still, and listen to Him. I am very blessed to be here today, more so, because I know I should be dead by now.

I do not deserve the love that I am blessed with, but I know that I am a child of God, and that He has forgiven me. And, I know my family had forgiven me too. I have the wonderful support of my family, and friends

that I have made in Christ. I love them all,
and thank them for not giving up one me.
Most of all I would like to thank God for
carrying me through the darkest times of my
life, and giving me the courage, and strength
to share my story in hopes that it might help
at least one person.
Thank you so much. Wendy

Wendy has been such a blessing to me. I have watched her go through battles and know where her strength comes from. She is now going into the county jail with me to do ministry. Wow! God is good! She has even gone a few times by herself. I see God growing in her, and she is giving her testimony to youth groups. Wherever God opens up a door for her she helps. She is the office manager at a Fortune 500 company that prepares taxes. I have started a training class for this tax season and I'm going to work for this company also. But to sit and listen to Wendy train us on how to prepare taxes blows my mind. She has come so far in just three years. And it hasn't all been easy for her either. She has had to fight treatments and I just received a text from her saying that her doctor's report was great and that she didn't have to go back for six months. Not only is she fighting for her life but her daughter has been in the children's hospital in Memphis trying to find out why she is having seizures. She has not given up, and we believe that God has healed her also.

In our journey it's not always peaches and cream, but it's who we trust, and who we have our eyes fixed on - Jesus

Yes, Lord
10

On December 31, 2010, I felt like Jacob. I wrestled with God all that night. Should I run for Justice Court Judge in the coming election? I never liked, or even knew anything about politics. But I knew it was in my spirit to run, and that's what I did for the next eight months. I believe God had a plan and purpose for me to run. During that time a door was opened for me to go into Central Mississippi Correctional Facility to be able to minister there. Wendy had started going with me to the county jail, and I knew if I became Judge I would no longer get to go into the county jail. So I felt one door was closing and another one was opening. Totally trusting in God that he wanted me to be the next Judge. In the primary election I got very few votes. My home community didn't even support me.

Jesus said, "A prophet is not without honor except in his own country, among his own relatives, and in his own house."
Mark 6:4

I was truly heart broken, not at the people, but this time at God. I was so frustrated. I didn't want to run for Judge. I didn't! I wrestled with Him not just that night, but the entire eight months. Because I knew that if I got that office I would have to answer to God, not to people, and it wouldn't matter if you had a dollar or a million, I would have to judge according to God's standards. I was angry. Why God did you want me to run! To make me look stupid one more time? I could do that all by myself I didn't need God to direct me in that.

Do you ever have a true conversion with God like this? I never had to this time either. I just knew he had all things worked out for those that loved the Lord and called according to his purpose. He does have His purpose, not mine!

I guess for a couple of weeks or longer I was talking to God about what the purpose was and all I heard was God keeps laying it on Godly people's heart to run for office, and they confess up front they are God fearing Christians, but it still people's choice who they vote for just like salvation. It's their choice to follow Jesus or not. My test was He asked me to run, and I obeyed. He never promised me the outcome.

Almost a year has passed since He placed that on my heart. It has been so hard for me to start writing again and I know that is my gift that is inside of me. It's not the English, or the grammar, but it's the gift inside my heart that he has given me to write and express my heart to others through the experience of my life and my journey.

I have had plenty of time to sit down to write, but for some reason I never would pick up my computer and start. I would pray for a job, an increase in bonding and my massage business. But I would feel in my spirit I should write, and everything in me couldn't do it. I could sit there and gaze at the walls an entire day. Day after day would pass and I would think why haven't you written? I would say tomorrow, or I will start next week.

As I have said I have had plenty of time to write, but day after day has gone by, it has been eight years since God laid this on my heart to do. This is my way that he wants me to minister to so many people, some I will never meet, but they will know my story. The hardest thing for me to realize is that he has called me to be an author. Wow; little old county girl back in the sticks with no education of writing. I was just trusting God, but it was so hard to grasp that. I needed a job. I needed money to support my Son and myself. When the finances would be there, then there would be something else to keep me from focusing on my calling.

At this very moment in my life I have four jobs that I'm working bonding, massage, working at a stockyard, and now working for a tax firm. And as of right now it's Christmas time, and I have no money to buy gifts for my kids' Christmas. My son is sixteen this year. The worse Christmas I can remember is when my brother got killed on November 30, 1979. I was sixteen, and we had no Christmas that year. We had presents but my mom didn't wrap them she just laid them on the chair and walked out of the room. I still have tears swell up in my eyes to think what she was going through.

My house payment is almost three months behind, and I need to buy groceries. Today I paid all the bills I could as far as the money would go. I know you think I mismanage my income, but I don't. I have little coming in. I hardly get any bonds anymore and very seldom get a call on massage. I only work one day at the stockyard, and I just got this tax job. I know in my heart that I'm to be writing.

I give all Glory and Honor to God that

before Christmas my house notes were paid and I had money to buy Christmas gifts not only for the kids but for others too.

I was awakened early this morning with "It's time" in my spirit. So from this day forward I am an author. That's my journey on this side…

Genie, a lady that came to our church for a short time. She is the one that had the open door for me to start doing ministry into our local prison, Central Mississippi Correction Facility. She has also given me permission to put her testimony in my book in hopes that it will minister to others.

I Thank God for Katrina
Hurricane Katrina was a storm that brought deadly destruction throughout the Gulf coast area in August 2005. Yet God used this storm to stop the destruction of my life and bring me back to Him. My story is not about someone who led a life of drug or alcohol addiction and then God drastically changed them. My story is about someone, who in the eyes of the world, led a very normal life, attending church and raising a family, yet I never had Jesus as Lord of my life. But God intervened and radically changed my life. I'm sharing this in hope that if others see themselves in my story, they will realize that only God's great love can fill that emptiness

inside.

I was raised by my grandparents in a godly home and attended all church events. I was basically a good little girl. I "joined" the church and was baptized when I was 9 or 10 years old because my big sister did. But the Holy Spirit convicted me during a revival in our little rural church when I was 16 years old. I knew I wasn't saved and accepted Christ as my Savior that night. I knew from then on that Jesus had saved me from all my sins and I began a journey with God, but it was short lived. When I turned 18, it was as if I became a totally different person.

I got involved with people who didn't know Jesus and before long I was wrapped up in the pleasures of the world, leaving Jesus out of my life. I got married at 17 and was divorced 5 months later. By the time I was 23, I had been married and divorced again. I had let go of the love of Jesus and tried to find love in worldly pleasures. I always knew God was there protecting me because I got myself in some situations that only God could get me out of unharmed. Occasionally I'd show up in church and repent, but then I'd go right back to my worldly ways.

One night when I left a party drunk, I had an accident, flipping my car three times. When someone stopped to pull me out of the vehicle that was upside down, I asked them to take me back to the party I had just left, leaving my car in the ditch. How crazy is that? Alcohol destroys rational thinking and brings utter destruction into one's life and their family's life. Yet alcohol has become the acceptable form of abuse in our society. It is what people do at office parties and many gatherings with friends and family. I know firsthand what alcohol does to a family; my father was an alcoholic who spent 4 years in prison. Yet I continued this type of life style for another 2 years. I was young and caught up in the world's short term pleasures.

I was very convicted over some of the things I did during those 7 years. Out of guilt, I started attending church and "rededicated" my life to the Lord. I did a lot of good things during this time to help others, but I still had no real relationship with Jesus.

I met a Christian man and got married for the third time and had 2 children. My career and family life were good. God had blessed me with a good job early in life and I climbed up the corporate ladder. We went to Sunday school and church every Sunday morning and made sure our boys were involved in all of the church activities. No Wednesday or Sunday night services though, we were too busy for that. Life seemed good.

Yet there was still something missing in

my life. I didn't have the peace and joy that I had as a young teenager when I accepted Jesus as my Savior. Even though we went to church every Sunday, attended Sunday school and a few church functions, God was not a part of our lives outside of church. We left God at church. Sure, we read bible stories to the boys and taught them a bedtime prayer and a blessing before meals, but that was about as far as we went. We did not have God as the center of our family and our marriage began to crumble.

After 17 years of marriage, I was once again divorced. I continued to go to church for a while only to keep the boys in church, but eventually quit going. I completely left Jesus out of my life again. The devil began to get a hold of me and my boys. I was not the strong single mother that everyone thought I was. I was miserable on the inside. The boys were struggling with the divorce and being teenagers as well. Life was not good.

God was tugging on my heart again. I began to visit some churches, but didn't go on a regular basis. I certainly didn't have a relationship with Jesus. During my time of searching for something in my life, hurricane Katrina struck. I became Red Cross certified and volunteered at one of the local church shelters. Two weeks after Katrina struck I had the opportunity to go to the Gulf Coast

*and work at the Disaster Recovery Center.
This is when my life began to change.*

*Volunteers from across the United
States were on the Gulf Coast to help. The
first three nights, I didn't even have a place to
stay and drove 6 hours each day back and
forth. Hotels rooms at one of the casinos
became available and I was able to stay on
the Gulf Coast for the next two weeks. We
didn't always have electricity or running
water and we had to shower with bottled
water. We worked at least 10 hours every day.
We worked with broken hearted people and
saw devastation everywhere. My heart broke
for the victims of hurricane Katrina.*

*We were emotionally exhausted at the
end of each day. Those of us who volunteered
because like family. I met a young man from
Oklahoma who I now know God sent there
specifically to minister to me. We talked
about our families which opened up the door
for this young man to talk to me about God.
He told me how he and his wife and another
young couple used to evangelize their
neighborhood. This was amazing to me. God
was a part of their family life. I had never had
that in a marriage.*

*We shared our life stories. He talked
about God a lot. God had stepped into his life
and drastically changed him. I had never
been around anyone who talked about God*

very much outside of church. Just listening to him talk I could tell there was something different about him. He had something that I didn't have and I wanted what he had. During one of our conversations he said "You need to get in a Spirit filled church." I didn't say much at the time, because I didn't really know what a "Spirit filled" church was. But I knew it wasn't the churches I had attended all my life. He told me that he and his family attended an Assembly of God church.

Over the next 3 months, I continued to volunteer at the Disaster Recovery Centers throughout south Mississippi. I began to listen to a Christian radio station the played contemporary Christian music. I had never heard this type of Christian music before. These were songs that spoke of broken people and the love of Jesus. Every song seemed to be written just for me. I began to pray and talk to God.

When I came back home, I looked up Assembly of God churches in my town. I had no idea what to expect, but I was determined to find out what a "Spirit filled" church was because they obviously had something that hadn't been in my previous churches. I mustered up enough courage to walk into unknown territory. I have never been greeted by so many friendly people who seemed to truly care about me. The church had a worship band that played the songs I heard on the radio. They truly worshipped the Lord and raised their hands and clapped. They took an interest in me and made sure I got connected with other people my age. People would get up from their seats and greet me when I walked in; I was accustomed to no one other than the front door greeters speaking to me in the other churches I had visited. This church had what my young friend from Oklahoma had. The love of Jesus was displayed through them! I liked this church.

They spoke about the Holy Spirit. The Holy Spirit was rarely mentioned in the other churches I had attended or maybe I just hadn't been listening. I knew about the Trinity; God the Father, the Son and the Holy Spirit. The believers in this church talked about a relationship with Jesus. These were things I had been missing all my life and I grew up in church and had attended church most of my adult life. How could I not know about the Holy Spirit? I had never had a real relationship with Jesus. I know I was saved when I was 16, but I too quickly got caught up in worldly pleasures to let my relationship with Jesus grow. I had never let the Holy Spirit act in my life. I never even knew He was there.

I continued to grow in this church. It seems I went to the altar, a crying mess, almost every Sunday and someone would pray with me. I thought you only went "down front" to be saved or to repent of some horrible sin. In this church we could go to the altar just to pray by ourselves and worship the Lord or have someone pray with us.

One Sunday at the altar, I totally surrendered my life to Jesus. I no longer wanted to live the empty life I had lived. I wanted Jesus to be Lord of my life. I wanted the Holy Spirit to be manifested in my life and guide. I wanted to love the Lord with all my heart, mind and soul. I wanted to be like Jesus. This wasn't done out of guilt this time, I wanted to love the Lord. I needed to learn how to do that. I told the Lord, "I am all yours, no turning back this time, have your way with my life" and I meant every word. The Holy Spirit revealed himself and I have never been the same since. I am a very different person today; filled with love, peace and joy. I desire to be in the presence of the Lord every day, every hour, every moment.

God has taken me on a journey with Him. Every day I'm learning to be more and more like Jesus. I'm learning to let God love others through me. God is breaking my heart for lost souls and broken hearted people. I don't always get it right and I still have trouble in this world, but my Jesus is bigger than anything the devil throws in my lap! I simply trust in the Lord.

God has called me into prison and jail and ministry and since then God has placed me in other churches where someone else has joined our prison ministry to share God's love with the broken hearted. Because I already loved someone who had been in prison, God knew that I would truly love others who are in prison. God knew I would share my story of being the daughter of someone in prison and that I would teach them about the freedom found only in Jesus and that I would show them the love of Jesus. Only Jesus can set them free while they are locked up. It is my passion and desire to see every lost soul come to know Jesus.

I truly regret that I took so long to let God be the center of my being and to have a loving deep relationship with Jesus and Holy Spirit. I wasted so many years that could l have spent in pure joy no matter what my circumstances.

So yes, I do thank God for Katrina. I'm sorry for the destruction and loss of lives, but I know God orchestrated every event in my life afterwards to put me at just the right place for the young man from Oklahoma to minister to me. I was not even supposed to be working at the Disaster Recovery Center where this young man was volunteering, but God caused a chain of events where I had to go that particular center.

Don't wait for God to send a major storm in your live before you start listening to Him. If you have not yet totally laid down your life and completely surrendered to the Lord, I encourage you to do so today. He is so worthy and you will be blessed beyond measure. The change in your life will be dramatic. God didn't create us to live mundane unhappy lives. He created us to love and to be loved and to share His great love with others. Let God love others through you. Let Him fulfill the calling He has on your life. Don't waste another moment on this earth. Let His deep love penetrate your every fiber. Doesn't just play church anymore, be the church? Holy Spirit will show you how!

Gift is within you
11

Last Sunday I got up, got my bath, put on my robe and looked outside. It was raining and cold. I just sat down in my chair gazing out into the cold thinking I'm not going to church today. I was almost back into my isolation mood, and I said, "No, you are going so get up and get dressed." We know when we don't feel like doing something that is when we going to miss our blessing. So I got ready to go to church. And yes it was my blessing.

Pastor preached on 2 Kings 4 Elisha, and the Widow's Oil, and how she had nothing left, and they were coming to get her two sons. When she went to Elisha, and he asked her what she had in her house, she said just a little oil. He told her to send her sons to borrow vessels, and to go into her house with her sons, and shut the door and pour the oil into the vessels. She didn't question the man of God. She needed a miracle, and the miracle was within her house. The house is within us. It is the gift that God has given each one of us. Pastor went on to tell us how hard it is and how he feels unworthy to preach, but he knows that this is his gift that God has given him.   Pastor said, "Kenneth, God has given you the gift of singing." At that time I asked God again was I still supposed to be writing because the money was not there and, I have bills and a child to take care of.

Let Pastor speak it if it is, Lord!

Before he closed his sermon he said, "Some of you are called to write just like the poem "Footprints in the Sand." I thank God my gift is still within me and God has a purpose for it.   And the poem, "My Child" at the beginning of this book. When I first wrote it, it was in my spirit to make it like "Footprint in the Sand" to take a picture like the cover of this book and put the poem with it. So I did.

People may make plans in their minds,
but the Lord decides what they will do.
                    Proverbs 16:9 NCV

Why do you think God's will for your life is so hard for our fleshly bodies to do? We know He has the very best in store for us, but we must manifest the gift He has given us.

Like a music box, if you don't wind it and lift the lid, no one will ever hear the music. The music will always be there. It's just stored in the box.

I love to write. It's when I feel the closest to God. The anointing is so strong. But then again it's so hard to do.   It is killing that flesh and coming into His will. Each book is just as hard to write because I so want it to be pleasing to Him and life touching and changing to you. I have wrestled with this writing for eight years now. I recall after I wrote my first book I had no idea that there would be other books. As I finished my first one, I remember thinking I would write ten more if I could have that closeness with God.

I was at a conference in New Boston,

Texas, when God gave one of our ministers a word to give to me and this scripture. I have kept them very close to my heart because it was confirmation to keep writing he said.

You whom I have taken from the ends of the earth, and called from its farthest regions, and said to you,
You are my servant; I have chosen you and have not cast you away:
Fear not, for I am with you; be not dismayed, for I am your God. I will strengthen you,
Yes, I will help you; I will uphold you with My righteous right hand.
'Behold, all those who were incensed against you shall be ashamed and disgraced; they shall be as nothing,
and those who strive with you shall perish.
You shall seek them and not find them-
Those who contended with you, those who war against you shall be as nothing, as a nonexistent thing.
For I, the Lord your God, will hold your right hand, saying to you, Fear not, I will help you.
Isaiah 41:9-13

I read it, and every time I read those five verses I am astonished, and my heart is so blown away by His promise that He is all I need. Such peace and comfort comes over me.

We have to have His word, His peace and comfort every day. We have to stay connected to the Father, or we have lost our joy, our purpose for this life. It's not about us. It's about our journey, our purpose for our lives to reach and touch others. We need to show love and compassion as Jesus did to us.

Final Journey
12

God has given me this chapter to conclude this book. We all will have a final journey just like the journey of our life. It all comes down to choice. Are we doing what God called us to do? Are we doing what we want to? If you are doing what you want to do, you're a man most miserable, looking for all the worldly goods that will rust away. Naked we come in this world and naked we will leave taking nothing with us, but our charter of who we really are. Who are you?

Are you a Christian who says God understands I'm not perfect; he made me like this? He gave me these sexual desires. I didn't mean to lie, it was for the best. That way no one gets hurt. Stand for what you believe in.
America is in the shape it is because we have

not taken a stand. I asked God to forgive me and change me, but He hadn't.

In Proverbs He tells us that it is better to be a Peacemaker than a Peacekeeper. We have to stand on what we believe and the way we feel. Sometimes we do things that we really don't want to do because we don't want to hurt someone's feelings, when all along we hurt them by lying to them.

He tells us to turn away from our wicked ways. We have to kill the flesh so the spirit man can live in us.

"But the cowardly, unbelieving, abominable, murderers, sexually immoral, sorcerers, idolaters, and all liars shall have their part in the lake which burns with fire and brimstone, which is the second death."
Revelation 21:8

It is that line that is in between when you were born and when you die that means so much. You only get the full effect of the line on your tombstone. Then it's too late to make any changes. Our choices are over. What is God's journey for you? Are you doing it, or are you allowing God to be a small part of your life? If I give Him too much I would have to surrender my life to Him and His desire for me. That's a sacrifice when he wants the very best for us.

If he will feed the birds of the air and the flowers of the field which are here today and gone tomorrow, how much more will He do for you when you are made in His own image?

I don't want people to remember that I worked hard and never could get ahead.
I had a hard life. I just seem to keep going around and around in circles.
I want my focus and my calling to be all about Jesus and what He did for me. I loved the Lord, and I gave back to the people.
It never mattered if you were rich or poor in my eyes. If I knew you, I loved you.
One thing I know. I was called by God to write, and I was a great author by the power of the Holy Spirit that guided me. I fulfilled my journey with what God wanted me to do.

One day all will know that I am looking in the face of Jesus.
That's all that matters is that day we are standing face to face with God Almighty and He says, "Well done my good and faithful servant." Then you know your journey is complete, but until that time we are to press on toward our high calling…

*"And He has made from one blood
every nation of men to dwell on all the face of
the earth, and has determined their
reappointed times and boundaries of their
dwellings, so that they should seek the Lord,
in the hope that they might grope for Him and
find Him, though He is not far from each one
of us; for in Him we live and move and have
our being, as also some of your own poets
have said, "For we are also His offspring."
"Therefore, since we are the offspring of
God, we ought not to think that the Divine
Nature is like gold or silver or stone,
something shaped by art and man's
devising."*

Acts 17:26-29

I know He has promised that one day
He will come back for us, and that there are
many mansions in My Father's house. The
streets are made of gold and the gates are
made with pearls. There will be no more tears
of sorrow. He will wipe the last tear away.
There will be no more pain, no more
suffering, no more sorrow. Eyes have not
seen the beauty that lies in wait for us in
heaven.

A time to be born, and a time to die.
Ecclesiastes 3:2

One of the greatest joy was helping take care of my cousin Julia. She had lung cancer and had given her life to the Lord and through her final days, I got to see what God's word meant when He said rejoice when one dies and cry when one is born. It makes so much sense if we are looking at it with spiritual eyes the way our Father sees everything.

Toward the end of her battle she never complained about hurting and she refused all medicine. I believe that her flesh was so near death that she wasn't hurting anymore. She was rejoicing for what she was seeing in the spirit. She would tell my aunt look the choir is in the front yard singing to me and then in a few minutes she would see them in the back yard. She was talking to different loved ones that had gone on. She was talking to Jesus, and we really didn't understand until she was gone the beauty and peace that she was experiencing before the end of her journey. I remember when she passed on, my aunt called me and I hurried right over so my aunt wouldn't be alone. Julia was so peaceful. The

home health nurse came and bathed her
before the funeral home took her and I helped
the nurse. It was such a peace not sadness.
We miss her and we will see her again along
with so many others that have gone on.
                    In Memory Of Julia

Don't think you will get there by being good, His word says different.

I know your works, that you are
neither cold nor hot. I could wish you were
cold or hot. So then, because you are
lukewarm, and neither cold or hot, I will
vomit you out of My mouth. Because you say,
I am rich, have become wealthy, and have
need of nothing' - and do not know that you
are wretched, miserable, poor, blind, and
naked.
                    Revelation 3:15-17

He starts this scripture off as I know your works. I know what you have done for the kingdom of God on earth. He wants us to be little Christians = Christ like. We are all a part of the body of Christ. If you are a born again child of God, you have a part to be doing - teaching, preaching, cooking, counseling, building, singing, writing, listening, proof reading, comforting, dancing. There are many parts; none is any better or bigger than the other. It is like the big toe. We have to have it to walk.

And if you don't know Jesus as your Lord and Savior, then you have chosen Satan as your father. There are no in between. Either you are a child of God or a child of Satan!

You have chosen the place that God had made for Satan and his angels. It's your choice not God's. He wants us all to come freely to him as a child trusting and loving their earthly Father. Some may have not had a great earthly Father that he could trust. It's hard to understand the unconditional love that God has for us. That's why we have to come to him as a child with a child's heart.

And I saw the dead, small and great, standing before God, and books were opened, which is the Book of Life. And the dead were judged according to their works, by the things which were written in the books.
And they were judged, each one according to his works. Then Death and Hades were cast into the lake of fire. This is the second death. And anyone not found written in the Book of Life was cast into the lake of fire.

Revelation 20:12-15

So at the end of our life what is your line going to say on your tombstone that matters?
He loved to party, she was a good person, they had it all!!!
Are as Apostle Paul said, "To live is Christ and to die is gain."

About the Author

She grew up in Sebastopol, a small town in central Mississippi. She was a sibling of three, being the youngest and only girl. They were brought up by their mother after their dad walked out on them. Wanda was only nine years old when this happened. Seven years later both of her brothers were killed six months apart. She lost her Dad ten years later.   Wanda lost her mom some twenty-three years later.

She is a single mother with two children and four grandchildren and a wonderful son-in-law. God has restored and blessed her so.

She is an ordained minister, author of two other books. You Are My Child, and All Messed Up. She goes into our local jail and ministers to the ladies and into the prison in Pearl, Ms.

She is a member of All Seasons Worship Center in Forest, Mississippi, where she and her son reside.